AUTHOR'S PREFACE

This little book is intended to introduce the reader to the joys of studying, keeping, and breeding the Burmese Python, *Python molurus bivittatus*, which is one of the most popular snake pets in the world.

even extinct in many of its former haunts. (In Hong Kong, where it was once common both in the wild and on the dinner table, it is now protected—at least in theory).

Another, probably more

The Burmese Python, *Python molurus bivittatus*, is undoubtedly one of the most popular snake pets in the world. Shown is a rare "Leopard" color variety, the product of selective breeding. Photo by David Dube.

Today we find ourselves in a fortunate situation—many snake species, including the Burmese Python, are being bred in captivity. This is important because many snakes (indeed, many reptiles overall) are still being killed for food, for skins, or through sheer ignorance, or hunted and collected for the pet trade. The Burmese Python is one of the most highly demanded sources of meat in the Far East gourmet food trade, such that it has become extremely rare,

dramatic, threat to many snake species is the loss of habitat through man's continuing clearance of the world's wilderness areas, ostensibly for "improvement." Thus, keeping and breeding Burmese Pythons in captivity is therefore a means of helping to preserve these fascinating creatures. And if this book helps that cause, then I will be more than satisfied.

John Coborn
Nanango, Queensland

INTRODUCING THE BURMESE PYTHON, *PYTHON MOLURUS BIVITTATUS*

In the following chapter we will be looking at certain natural aspects of Burmese Python. Although the facts given are not essential for you to successfully maintain and even breed Burmese Pythons in captivity, you should regard this information as background knowledge to your chosen hobby, which will surely enhance your enjoyment and lead you on the way to becoming a

Facing page: The Burmese Python is currently listed as a threatened species (Appendix II) by the Convention on the International Trade in Endangered Species (CITES), which means all specimens imported or exported require special permits. Photo by Isabelle Francais, courtesy of Bill Brant.
Below: Average adult length for the Burmese Python is somewhere around 15 ft/450 cm, but some have been known to reach as long as 18 ft/540 cm. Shown is a beautiful albino specimen. Photo by David Dube.

The Burmese Python is native to southern Asia. Many of the specimens that had been imported into the United States originally came from Thailand. Photo by Isabelle Francais.

serious amateur herpetologist.

BASIC FACTS

Burmese Pythons are cold-blooded and thus must rely on their environment for bodily warmth. A wild Burmese Python, for example, may live inside a hollow tree limb, the upper part of which is exposed to the sun all day (the warm part), the lower part being down in the shade (the cool part); and the snake just needs to move up or down as necessary. Of course, this system does not work at night and pythons would mainly be active at night only during the warmer months (when temperatures stay over 68°F/20°C at night).

Burmese Pythons are wholly carnivorous, taking prey compatible with their size. Due to their low metabolic rate, they do not require the food quantities needed by the higher animals, but a Burmese Python will obviously take a substantial meal considering its relatively large size.

MORPHOLOGY AND PHYSIOLOGY

The ventral scales of Burmese Pythons are many times larger and broader than those on the rest of the body. This single row of large scales plays a major part in the snake's locomotion. Snake locomotion is a complex and interesting subject. Burmese Pythons usually move with a combination of "snaking" and "rectilinear crawling." When snaking, the Burmese Python advances by making a series of lateral curving motions, using solid objects such as stones, branches, tufts of grass, etc., for leverage with the rear part of the curves, in order to push itself forward. With rectilinear crawling the snake uses its broad belly scales which are in contact with the substrate; through a complicated system of muscle contractions, the snake "walks" on its jointed ribs, pushing itself over the ground via the ventral scales.

Because a snake needs to be very versatile in its body movements it has a large number of sophisticatedly jointed vertebrae, each with an attached pair of ribs. Compared with the meager 33 bones contained in the human backbone, the Burmese Python has in excess of 350!

A Burmese Python's sense of smell is very highly developed and is closely involved with the two-pronged forked tongue that is continually flickering in and out through an opening (the labial notch) located on the tip of the upper half of the mouth. When the tongue is flickered out it picks up scent particles which are taken into the mouth and transferred to a pair of pits in the roof of the mouth. These are the openings to a very efficient sensing organs known as the Jacobson's organ(s), which are literally for smelling the contents of the air. These organs are situated in the palate below the nostrils but they form separate chambers lined with extremely sensitive membranes and work independently of the nasal sense of smell. The eyes of the Burmese Python have vertical pupils, which is not unusual in nocturnal

Thanks to the efforts of captive breeders, Burmese Python enthusiasts can now appreciate such unique specimens as this "Green Phase" Burmese Python. Photo by K. H. Switak.

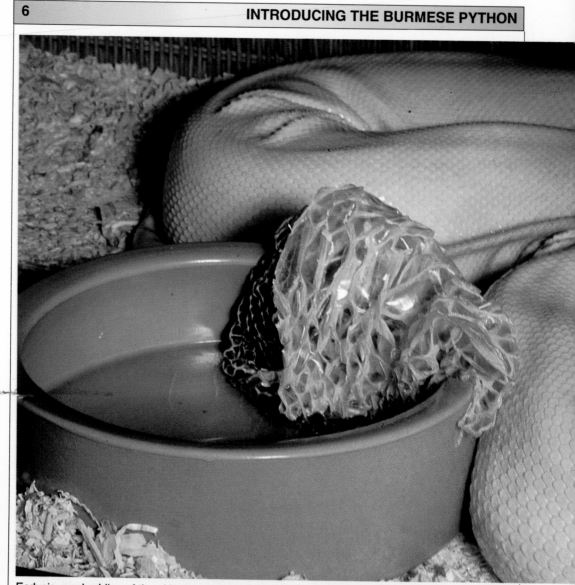

Ecdysis, or shedding of the skin, is a normal part of every snake's life. It is important that captive specimens shed their skin in one neat piece, or, at the very least, in only a few broken pieces. Photo by Isabelle Francais, courtesy of Bill Brant.

snakes. Other adaptations that probably occurred during the period of subterranean development include a highly efficient means of detecting odors and a very acute sense of touch.

RANGE

The Burmese Python occurs naturally in northeastern India, Burma, Indo-China, and southern China as far as Hong Kong, as well as Thailand, the Malaysian Peninsula, and some of the Indonesian Islands. It occurs in a wide range of habitats, from open woodland to rainforest. It usually lives in areas where good cover is available, such as in thick vegetation or on boulder strewn hillsides and river banks, and never too far away from water. It is an adept climber and spends varying amounts of time among tree branches or on the ground. It loves to bathe in water during hot weather, completely immersing itself with the obvious exception of the nostrils to breathe through.

EVOLUTION AND CLASSIFICATION

Although snakes are thought to have evolved from burrowing lizards, there are no modern reptiles that show an intermediate phase, so the burrowing concept can only be regarded as theory until we can prove otherwise by finding the right fossils or by some other sophisticated means yet to be developed. In the meantime we must continue to conjecture about the true evolutionary story of our friend the Burmese Python.

The Reptilia, the Class to which

Burmese Pythons have the scientific name *Python molurus bivittatus* and share the species with only one other snake, the Indian Python, *Python molurus molurus*. Some people believe there is a third snake, the Sri Lankan Python, *P. m. pimbura*, but the majority of taxonomists consider it to be nothing more than another form of the Indian Python and thus unworthy of subspecies recognition. Photo by Isabelle Francais, courtesy of Eugene L. Bessette.

the Burmese Python and all other reptiles belong, is a group of vertebrate animals intermediate between the fishes and amphibians on one side, and the higher vertebrates (the birds and the mammals) on the other.

The Burmese Python is a subspecies of the Indian Python, which has the scientific name of *Python molurus*, *Python* being the genus and *molurus* being the specific part of the name. As

Python (or Light-Phase Indian Python). Its scientific name is *Python molurus bivittatus*, while that of its aforementioned close relative is *Python molurus molurus*.

Pythons form the subfamily

Kingdom: Animalia (all animals)

Phylum: Vertebrata (Craniata) (all backboned animals)

Class: Reptilia (all reptiles)

Order: Squamata (lizards and snakes)

Suborder: Serpentes (all snakes)

Family: Boidae (pythons and boas)

Subfamily: Pythoninae (all pythons)

Genus: *Python* (typical pythons)

Species: *Python molurus* (Indian Pythons)

Subspecies 1: *P. m. molurus* (Indian Python) (nominate)

Subspecies 2: *P. m. bivittatus* (Burmese Python)

Subspecies 3: *P. m. pimbura* (Ceylon Python– questionable)

---

there are also other species in the genus, these are given different specific names (for example: *Python regius*, *Python reticulatus*, and *Python sebae*). In some cases a subspecific name may be added to the binomial, making it a trinomial. This is the case when two geographical races of a species are different but not different enough to warrant separate specific status. The subject of this book, the Burmese Python (or Dark-Phase Indian Python, as it is known to some) is a capital example of this. It is a subspecific relative of the Indian

Pythoninae in the reptilian family Boidae, which includes six more subfamilies: Boinae (typical boas); Bolyerinae (Round Island boas); Calabarinae (Calabar Ground Python); Erycinae (Rubber Boa, Rosy Boa, and sand boas); Loxoceminae (Mexican Dwarf Boa); and Tropidophinae (wood, or dwarf, boas). Perhaps the best way to view the position of the Burmese Python in zoological classification is to look at a hierarchical table. We know that the python is an animal as opposed to a plant so we will start there. See chart above.

ACCOMMODATING YOUR PYTHONS

Pet snakes are kept in a terrarium, vivarium, cage, or whatever you wish to call it (I will refer to it from here on as the first one, the terrarium). There are no hard and fast rules concerning terrarium construction as long as the basic life-support systems are correct. At one time the best idea of a terrarium was a box with a glass front, heated with a light-bulb. These days, however, terrarium technology has advanced considerably. Now you can buy ready made cages with all the apparatus built right in. These cages may be made from fiberglass, metal, or timber.

THE GLASS TERRARIUM

Juvenile Burmese Pythons will be quite at home in a fish tank full of air instead of water. A tank that is 36 in long x 18 in wide x 18 in high (90 cm long x 45 cm wide x 45 cm high) will be adequate for a pair of juveniles until they are about 4 ft/120 cm long. Remember that

There is a large variety of tank sizes at your disposal, all of which can be used to house Burmese Pythons. For particularly large specimens, you can order custom-made tanks. Photo courtesy of Hagen.

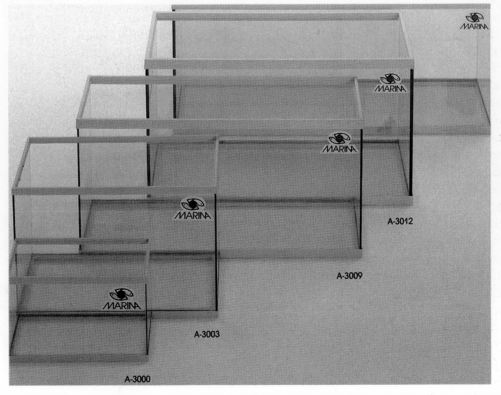

For smaller Burmese Pythons, you may want to consider buying a tank top and a light in one convenient piece. The flip-top lid also makes it easy to drop in food items, change waterbowls, etc. Photo courtesy of Hagen.

snakes rarely stretch themselves out fully when resting and if well-fed will not be overtly active. They will get adequate exercise from regular handling sessions.

The tank must, of course, have a secure but well-ventilated lid. It is prudent to make this a box-like structure in which the heating and lighting apparatus can be affixed. The apparatus must be separated from the snakes with strong metal mesh. This will prevent them from getting in and burning themselves.

THE WOODEN TERRARIUM

As they grow, your pythons will require larger accommodations. Many hobbyists graduate to glass-fronted wooden terrarium at this stage. Such cages are very versatile and can be made to a shape or size ready to fit almost anywhere. They can be free standing or constructed as a permanent fixture in an alcove. The glass access and viewing panels can be framed or unframed, hinged or sliding, but be sure not to leave any gaps through which snakes can escape. Even a fairly stout python can manage to wriggle through a surprisingly narrow gap!

Some hobbyists are very inventive when it comes to terrarium construction, and excellent cages are often made from old closets, wardrobes, TV cabinets, and so on. A large display cabinet, for example, could easily be modified, maybe with a strengthening of the floor and attention to waterproofing. It may help to look in your local thrift shop to see what they have lying around.

Once your Burmese Pythons reach 4 ft/120 cm or more in length it is best to construct a cage of a size that will be suitable for them for the rest of their lives, otherwise you will be building a bigger cage every time they grow another foot or two! I would suggest that an adult Burmese requires a cage that is at least 6 ft long x 3 ft wide x 6 ft high (200 cm long x 100 cm wide x 200 cm high), and remember you will need at least two of these if you are going to breed your snakes (keeping male and female separate outside the breeding

Keeping a Burmese Python's tank clean is an absolute necessity. All keepers should design a routine cleaning schedule and stick to it. Photo by Isabelle Francais, courtesy of Eugene L. Bessette.

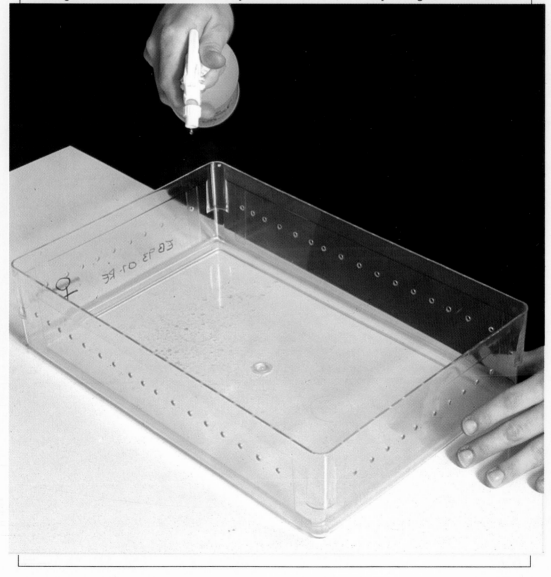

Above; Wood shavings are a reasonable substrate for Burmese Pythons, but be sure not to use shavings of the cedar variety, for the oils will irritate their skins. Photo by Isabelle Francais, courtesy of Bill Brant. **Facing page:** Do not simply pour old water out of a bowl and then refill it; clean the bowl first. Dirty water can lead a Burmese Python to many illnesses. Photo by Isabelle Francais, courtesy of Eugene L. Bessette.

season will enhance chances of successful mating when they are introduced). To make a substantial wooden terrarium the best material is undoubtedly .5 in/10 mm plywood. Chipboard, blockboard, or hardboard can also be used but these are more prone to dampness than plywood and have to be treated with primer, undercoat, and at least two coats of good quality, non-toxic gloss paint for protection. Fiberglass resin is also an excellent waterproofer for such materials. Even plywood should be given a couple of coats of exterior marine varnish or a coat of fiberglass resin to protect it from the dampness caused when the snakes enter and leave their water baths.

TERRARIUM HEATING

Burmese Pythons will require supplementary heating in all areas outside the tropics. The air temperature in the cage should be maintained at 79 to 86°F/26 to 30°C during the day, reducing to around 68°F/20°C at night. In most homes, you will not require any additional supplementary heating in the terrarium so you simply switch the heating apparatus off for the night and on again in the

Newspaper is another excellent substrate to use with Burmese Pythons. It is economical, disposable, and easy to work with. Photo by Isabelle Francais, courtesy of Eugene L. Bessette.

Facing page: Building your own enclosures can be an immensely rewarding undertaking. If you decide to do this, be sure to make the front pieces completely removable so to afford yourself easy access inside. Photo by Isabelle Francais, courtesy of Eugene L. Bessette.

Keeping careful and accurate records of all your snakes' doings is a very important part of being a good herpetoculturist. Sheddings, defecations, feedings, etc., are all events that should be written down. Photo by Isabelle Francais, courtesy of Eugene L. Bessette.

Facing page: Small Burmese Pythons can be kept in number in a well-organized rack system like the one shown here. Although a commercial setup like this one takes much time and effort to create, many conveniences are afforded the keeper. Photo by Isabelle Francais, courtesy of Eugene L. Bessette.

morning. You should use a reliable thermometer so that you can monitor the temperature regularly, and it is preferable to have a thermostat so you can regulate the temperature automatically.

There are many kinds of heating apparatus available. For the fish tank terrarium as described above, ordinary domestic tungsten light bulbs can be used. You can experiment with wattages, but a couple of 75-watt bulbs operated with a thermostat should be adequate for a tank of the size described for juvenile Burmese Pythons. The bulbs should be installed in the box-lid, behind the wire mesh. They should be placed at one end of the cage only so that a temperature gradation is created from one end of the tank to the other. This will mean that.

Under-tank heating pads are among the most sensible and effective products one can use to help a Burmese Python maintain warmth. They are available in many pet shops and are offered in a number of sizes and wattages. Photo courtesy of Zoo Med.

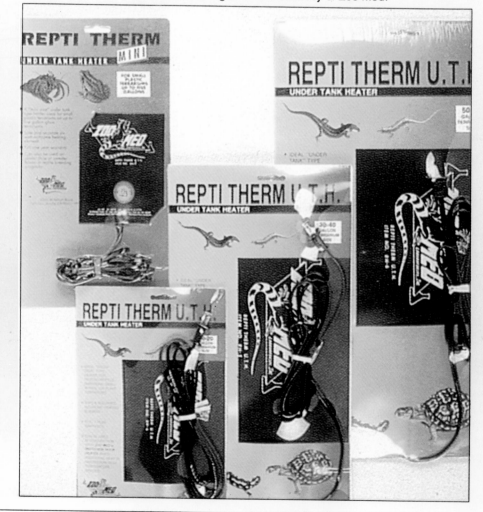

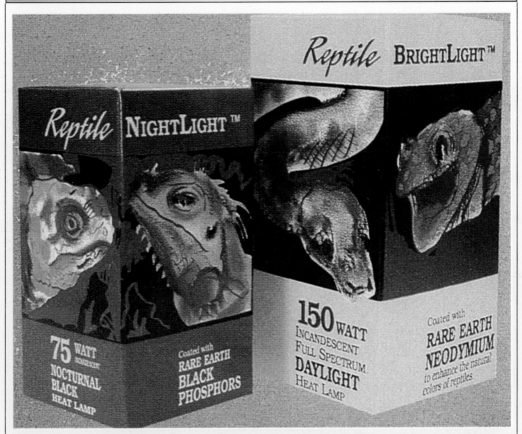

In order to correctly replicate a Burmese Python's photoperiod (day/night cycle), you should invest in a set of bulbs specially designed for just this purpose. Photo courtesy of Energy Savers.

a snake can move from warmer to cooler spots in the tank, and vice versa, to suit itself. If you need to apply some heat at night (such as when you keep your cage in an unheated garage or outhouse), you can supply warmth without excessive light by having a low-wattage blue–or red-colored bulb. These are used at night only to keep the chill out.

In larger cages you will require more substantial heating. Large (150-watt and higher) infra-red lamps and tubular steel heaters come to mind. There are several kinds of heaters on the market, so perhaps you should look around and see what's available. It is best to have any heater operated by a thermostat, and ensure that your Burmese Pythons cannot get into direct contact with them. Some snakes have received severe burns by coiling around heaters.

LIGHTING

Although Burmese Pythons are naturally nocturnal, they are still influenced by photoperiod (the cycles of day and night) so their cages must be adequately lit during the day.

Heated rocks are a sensible product for the provision of reptile warmth. These can be found at most any pet shop that stocks other herpetocultural supplies, and they are usually very reasonably priced. Photo courtesy of Zoo Med.

Changes in photoperiod will increase breeding successes as described in the breeding chapter. There are several makes of fluorescent tubes available that emit a "daylight"

Keeping tabs on a Burmese Python's ambient temperature is essential. If, for whatever reason, the temperature slips too low or too high, you could very well end up with a sick snake. Photo courtesy of Hagen.

quality of light. These can be used in conjunction with any other forms of heat lamps to provide excellent lighting. These lamps also emit small amounts of ultra-violet light that will enhance and improve the general health of your snakes.

CAGE FURNISHINGS

Cage furnishings for large snakes should be as simple as possible. The simpler they are, the easier it will be to maintain good hygiene. Your pythons will require a floor covering, a water bath, a branch on which they can climb, and somewhere they can hide.

Absorbent paper towels or newspapers can be used for juvenile snakes. As soon as the towels are soiled they can be removed and replaced. Larger snakes can have a substrate of coarse gravel, to be changed and washed at regular intervals. Some hobbyists have made good use of artificial grass, bath towels, or old pieces of carpet.

To add a little "visual spice" to a Burmese Python's tank, you should consider obtaining a scenic sheet that can be attached to the back wall. Photo courtesy of Creative Suprizes.

By having a spare set of any of these, you can change them at regular intervals and wash the soiled ones.

The water bath should be large enough for the python to completely immerse itself without the water overflowing, otherwise you will have flooding problems. Of course, if you have a concrete floor and drainage system, all the better.

The climbing branch or branches must be strong enough to support the snakes and must be secured to the floor and wall to prevent them from slipping. It is good to find unusually shaped branches. You can do this by going out and looking for fallen timber in the woods, along river banks, or on the sea shore. Those logs found on the latter will have been exposed to the sun, sand, and water and will have been bleached and smoothed. Such branches are very attractive.

Burmese Pythons are less stressed if they are in close contact with the environment, especially when resting. That is why they like to squeeze themselves fairly tightly into hollows and cavities. In the wild they will use hollow limbs and branches, both on living and fallen trees, plus rock crevices or burrows of other animals. A juvenile Burmese Python would of course like a hollow branch in its tank, but it will find a shoebox or cereal carton quite satisfactory as well. You can easily change this each time it gets dirty.

If you have an enclosure that is large enough, you will undoubtedly want to consider adding a few large branches into the setup of any particularly large Burmese Pythons. Remember, however, that soiled wood is very hard to keep clean; you may have to replace these branches frequently. Photo by B. Kahl.

To accommodate large specimens you can make a resting shelf about half way up the wall of the terrarium in the rear corner. This consists of a wooden shelf with an edge at least 8 in/20 cm high all around it. You can even cover part of the top to give the snake the illusion of being enclosed, but be sure to leave a substantial part of the top open so that you can always see the snake and gain easy access to it if necessary.

For small Burmese Pythons, say, about seven feet and under, you will be able to find glass aquariums of appropriate size in which to house them, but when those animals start getting in the nine and ten foot range, you should consider giving them something considerably more substantial, like a large, hand-built cage or perhaps even a whole room. Photo by Mella Panzella.

Burmese Pythons are climbers, but they also like to occasionally hide. It is important that they be given a place to go where they will feel safe and solitary. Photo by David Dube.

FEEDING AND FOODS

Reports of what the wild Burmese Python eats are few and far between. We do know that they are fairly opportunistic, meaning they are likely to grab anything they can overpower. There are reports of large Burmese Pythons eating small deer, monkeys, jackals, and even leopards, as well as several kinds of domestic mammals and birds, including goats, pigs, dogs, cats, chickens, and ducks. Smaller prey includes various birds, rats, other rodents, and even fish, though I have never heard of a captive specimen accepting the latter.

A typical prey-catching sequence in the life of a wild

Facing page: Burmese Pythons are very eager feeders. Soon you may find your own specimens looking eagerly out of their tanks while awaiting their next meal. Photo by Isabelle Francais, courtesy of Bill Brant. **Below:** Burmese Pythons are aggressive hunters that spend their daytime hours searching for just about anything they can grab hold of. Some large specimens have been known to take deer, monkeys, and even leopards. If you are the type who believes in letting your Burmese Python roam free, keep it away from your cat or dog! This is not a joke! Photo by M. J. Cox.

Burmese Python could be described as follows: the snake is initially attracted to a prey animal, perhaps a large squirrel, maybe by the animal's movement (by seeing it or detecting its vibrations). As soon as the "thought" of a prospective meal arises, the snake will become excited, flickering its tongue as it endeavors to pick up scent particles. The heat sensory pits in the lips will also play their part in

Facing page; The best type of gloves to wear with specimens that you know are "biters" are those of the rubber variety, as used in kitchens. Snakes have trouble latching onto these gloves and apparently don't care for the taste of them either. Photo by Isabelle Francais, courtesy of Bill Brant.

When you have a specimen that you know to be particularly nasty, it is best you feed it with a gloved hand. Photo by Isabelle Francais, courtesy of Bill Brant.

Burmese Pythons are not known for their gentleness when attacking their prey. Some keepers may find this somewhat unpleasant to watch. Photo by Isabelle Francais, courtesy of Bill Brant.

Many keepers prefer to offer food items that have already been killed. Even if you do this, chances are a Burmese Python will go through the process of constricting it anyway. Photo by Isabelle Francais, courtesy of Bill Brant.

ascertaining that it is indeed warm-blooded prey and further inform the snake of its suitability for food.

Having recognized the prey and pinpointed its position with a combination of the senses, the snake will slowly and stealthily approach the animal until it can get itself in a position suitable for striking (sometimes the prey animal will conveniently pass right into the snake's range of strike, thus saving the snake a

Facing page: Mice are probably the food item most often given to captive Burmese Pythons. Shown here are a pile of "fuzzies," which can be offered in quantity to very young snakes. Photo by Isabelle Francais, courtesy of Tom Crutchfield.

It is best for a Burmese Python to grab and swallow its prey head first. Sometimes a snake that has grabbed its prey tail first (or even worse, by the sides) will have trouble getting it down. Photo by Isabelle Francais, courtesy of Bill Brant.

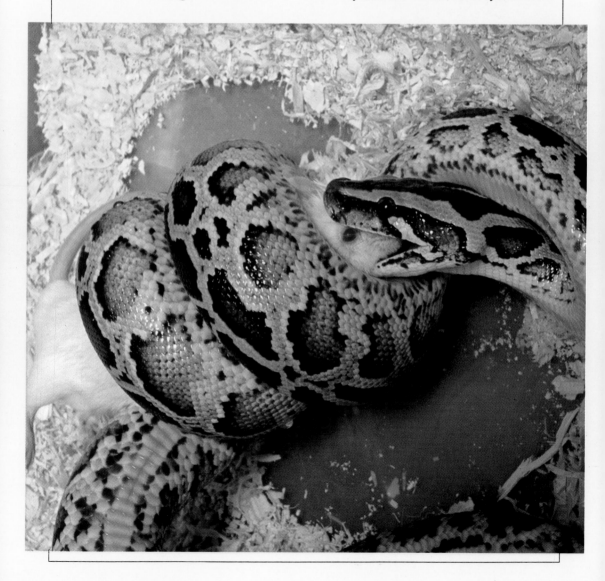

certain amount of work!). The Burmese Python may hunt in trees or on the ground. As soon as the prey is in range the snake will draw the first third of its body into an "S" shape while drawing the rear part of the body forward ready to throw coils. The snake launches its head forward, simultaneously opening its mouth and grabbing the prey. The prey may be grasped anywhere on its body, the python's numerous recurved teeth preventing it from getting away.

At the same time, the python throws several coils of its body around the prey item and squeezes hard with its powerful muscles. This will cause the prey animal to gasp for air. Each time it does this, the python increases the pressure. The prey is not "crushed" as such, but enough pressure is applied to stop the animal breathing. In other words, the prey is quickly killed by suffocation combined with shock.

When taking prey that could be considered dangerous (rats and

T. F. H. Publications offers a very wide range of specialized reptile and amphibian books. Each book is highly authoritative and fully illustrated in color. These books are available at pet shops everywhere.

mice are prime examples), a snake uses its efficient sense of touch and its coils to maneuver the head of the prey into a position in which the prey is not given the opportunity to bite. Once the prey is dead, the snake loosens its grip and begins to examine it with its tongue in order to locate the head.

front of the lower jawbones are connected with elastic tissue enabling the left and right jaw to spread open. In order to avoid damage to the brain while the python is swallowing large prey, the skull is complete, tough, and movable. Finally, the tissues of the gut, the flesh, and the skin

One aspect of Burmese Python keeping that an enthusiast should be aware of is the fact that most Burmese Pythons have a voracious appetite. Large specimens can be very costly to feed. Photo by B. Kahl.

A Burmese Python will almost always start swallowing at the head end of the prey.

It is a well known fact that virtually all snakes are capable of swallowing prey many times larger than their own heads. To do this the snake has several adaptations. The lower jaw is not hinged rigidly to the skull but is attached by elastic ligaments that allow a huge gape when the jaw is virtually "unhinged." Also, the

are highly elastic to allow accommodation of large prey.

Once a Burmese Python has found the snout of its prey, swallowing begins. If you watch this process you will see that the prey seems to stay in one spot while the snake engulfs it, moving forward over its body with its head and jaws, the latter working one side and then the other as the prey slowly disappears into the snake's gullet. Once the prey has

been forced through the neck region, it is moved more speedily into the stomach by peristaltic muscle action.

After a heavy meal, a Burmese Python will need to rest for a week or so to digest it. It is important that temperatures are optimum during this time or digestion problems may otherwise ensue. In the wild, the snake will retreat into a sun-warmed refuge where it will rely on its camouflage to remain unnoticed by predators (including man).

To keep your captive Burmese Python in the best of health it will require a balanced diet containing proteins, fats, carbohydrates, vitamins, and minerals. That is a golden rule of herptile feeding—variety is truly beneficial. If you can provide it, do so.

Some fanciers like to breed their own food items for their snakes, but this tends to take up as much or even more time than tending the snakes themselves. Also, you would need to learn how to care for the food animal, bearing in mind that even if it is only snake-food it must still be kept in kind and humane conditions!

The following are the items on which captive Burmese Pythons are largely fed:

Mice: Mice are available from pet shops and sometimes as

Facing page: Being arboreal, Burmese Pythons also include birds in their diet. A few birds you may able to offer your Burmese Python are chickens, guinea hens, quail, and other assorted domestic fowl. Photo by P. J. Stafford.

surplus from medical laboratories. They may be white or colored but that does not seem to make much difference as far as the snake is concerned. Some companies are now supplying bulk quantities of freshly killed and frozen mice which can be kept in a deep-freeze until needed. Allow a good 12 hours for the mice to reach room temperature before feeding them to your snakes, or, if you need them in a hurry, place them in a cup of hot water (not boiling water). Mice are suitable for young Burmese from hatchling size to about 3 ft/90 cm.

Rats: Rats can be obtained on a similar basis to mice. Pythons graduate to medium sized rats at about 3 ft/90 cm in length. Of course, young rats can be fed to smaller pythons and large rats to larger pythons.

Chickens: Domestic fowl, from hatchling to adult, can be used for pythons of various sizes. However, day-old chicks are not as nutritious as those which have been feeding for a few days so day-olds should be fed along with mice or young rats to juvenile pythons. Such chicks can also be bought in bulk, deep frozen. You may be able to obtain surplus live day-old chicks from your local hatchery and these can be kept and grown to sizes suitable for your snakes. Fully-grown, large varieties of domestic fowl are suitable usually only for adult pythons in excess of 10 ft/3 m.

Other Foods: Quails, pigeons,

ducks, guinea fowl, guinea pigs, and rabbits will all have their uses if available, but please do heed the warning about being kind and humane to such animals.

FREQUENCY OF FEEDING

It is not easy to say how often a Burmese Python should be fed, but it is better to give too little than too much. Burmese Pythons kept in optimum conditions are rarely shy when there is a hint of food and many will eat just about as much as you are willing to give them. Unfortunately, captive Burmese are very prone to obesity, a condition in which many of the body organs become almost inoperative due to the enormous fat deposits that build up in and around them. Fat pythons also do not breed well!

A hatchling python will often not feed until after its first molt, which can be up to one week after hatching. It will then usually take a dead mouse that is jiggled about in front of it. For the first three months you can give it maybe two mice a week for a good start, but thereafter reduce to three every two weeks. When the snake reaches about 3 ft/90 cm in length at six to eight months, it will graduate to medium-sized rats. One per week will be adequate; the same goes for larger prey as the snake matures. Very large specimens will do quite well on a large chicken, duck, or rabbit about once every two weeks. Once accustomed to taking dead prey, most Burmese Pythons will accept it automatically without any further need to encourage it.

FORCE-FEEDING

Sometimes a snake will refuse to feed for no apparent reason or it will refuse because it is sick or has been sick. You must treat the snake for its sickness before or in conjunction with force-feeding. There are two ways of force-feeding a Burmese Python. The first is to take a whole dead prey animal (it is easier with a mouse or rat rather than with a chicken) of suitable size. Next take the snake by the neck and open its mouth by pulling gently but firmly at the loose skin under the snake's jaw. When its mouth is sufficiently open, introduce the head of the prey animal and push it into the gullet as far as you can. Sometimes the snake will start swallowing of its own accord at this stage. If necessary, use something firm, but not too hard, like the lubricated (in mineral oil) handle of a wooden spoon. Once it is past the neck region you can usually massage the prey down into the stomach with your hand.

Another way is to use an instrument like a large syringe and pump liquid food into the animal. The stomach tube to which it is attached should have a smooth end and should be lubricated with mineral oil. You can also use a stomach tube thick enough to take a whole mouse. The lubricated tube is passed slowly into the snake's gullet and the mouse pushed down the tube with a plunger. Before you try any of these methods you are advised to obtain instruction from a veterinarian or experienced enthusiast.

To make record-keeping as convenient for yourself as possible, keep the chart attached to the enclosure itself. Photo by Isabelle Francais, courtesy of Eugene L. Bessette.

SOME MEDICAL ASPECTS

Pythons kept in optimum conditions and fed regularly are unlikely to become sick, but it is advisable to be aware of what to do in the unfortunate event of a disease outbreak. If your python should become sick and you do not know what is wrong with it then you need to consult a veterinarian. Many veterinarians today are taking an interest in the more exotic pets; there are some who specialize in reptile health. Even if your local vet is unsure about snakes he will most likely be able to put you in contact with someone who is.

The following is a brief list of the more common conditions and diseases that your Burmese Python may encounter:

Nutritional Problems: Not usually a problem with Burmese that are fed on animals that have been raised on a balanced diet. In cases of vitamin deficiency (due to feeding on nutritionally substandard, day-old chicks for example), fluid vitamin/mineral supplement can be injected into the dead prey animal before feeding it to the snake. Sometimes your vet may recommend the introduction of concentrated nutrients and/or medicines to the stomach of a snake that is being treated for a disease. This will be administered via a stomach tube.

Wounds and Injuries: Though not strictly diseases, wounds caused by fighting, attempting to escape, lamp or heater burns, etc., are all susceptible to infection and must be treated. Shallow wounds will usually heal automatically if swabbed daily with a mild antiseptic such as povidone-iodine. Deeper or badly infected wounds should be dealt with by a veterinarian since in some cases surgery, suturing, and antibiotic treatment may be required.

Ticks and Mites: These are the most common external parasites associated with snakes. Ticks are often found attached to newly captured reptiles, though they are rare in captive-bred specimens. Ticks range up to .25 in/5 mm in length. They fasten themselves to the snake with their piercing mouthparts, usually in a secluded spot between scales (often around the vent or under the chin). Do not attempt to pull a tick directly out because its head may snap off and remain in the skin, causing an infection later on. The tick's body should first be dabbed with a little alcohol (surgical spirit or even whiskey) to relax the mouthparts. The tick can then be gently pulled out with thumb and forefinger or with forceps.

Mites are more of an infestation of captive snakes than of wild ones. A heavy mite infestation can be regarded as serious; mites can often multiply to large numbers in the terrarium before they are even noticed. They do not necessarily stay on a reptile's bodies all of the

Above: Removing a tick from a snake can be a very delicate affair; it requires the proper instruments and a steady hand. If you do not think you can handle this procedure efficiently, bring your snake to either a vet or a more experienced herpetoculturist. Photo by William B. Allen, Jr. **Below:** Any kind of severe wound will have to be treated by a veterinarian. In many cases, the wound will have to be sutured, like the one shown here, which was caused by a fight with a cagemate. Photo by William B. Allen, Jr.

time but may instead hide in crevices in the terrarium. In great numbers, mites can cause stress, anemia, sloughing problems, loss of appetite, and even death. They are also capable of transmitting blood pathogenic organisms from one reptile to another. The individual reptile mite is smaller than a pinhead, roughly globular in shape, and grayish in color, becoming red after it has partaken of a blood meal. In a heavily infested terrarium, the mites may be seen running over the surfaces (particularly at "lights-on" in the mornings) and their tiny, silvery, powdery droppings may be seen on a Burmese Python's skin. Mites are most often introduced to the terrarium with new stock (another good reason for quarantine and careful inspection).

Mites can be quickly eradicated using insecticidal dichlorvos strip (of the type used to control houseflies). A small piece of such a strip placed in a perforated container and suspended in the terrarium will kill off the offending creatures. Remove the strip after three days then repeat the operation ten days later to kill off any newly hatched mites. Two or three treatments will usually destroy all mites involved.

Worm Infections: There are many species of worms that can internally infect Burmese Pythons. The ones with which we are most likely to be concerned are roundworms and tapeworms. Nearly all wild snakes are infected with worms of one form or

another, but in most cases there is no danger to the reptiles. However, during times of stress (capture, unsuitable heating, starvation, and other diseases, for example), normal resistance to the worms may be reduced, triggering a massive increase in size or numbers of worms, causing anemia, general lethargy, loss of appetite, and eventual death. Routine microscopic examination of fecal samples in a veterinary laboratory will reveal infestations. There are several proprietary brands of vermicides available through your veterinarian which may be offered with the food, or in severe cases via stomach tube.

Bacterial Infections: there are many forms of bacterial infections which can infect pythons. Infective salmonellosis is an intestinal disease which has been known to have been transmitted from reptiles to man (especially so from freshwater turtles) so it is important to thoroughly wash the hands after each cleaning or handling session. In pythons, salmonellosis manifests itself in the watery, green-colored, foul-odored feces. Consult a veterinarian who will probably treat the infection with an antibiotic drug.

Facing page: Dealing with any oral infections will require very gentle treatment. In this photo, the keeper is opening the mouth with a cotton swab, which is much more preferable to, say, a metal probe. Photo by Isabelle Francais, courtesy of Bill Brant.

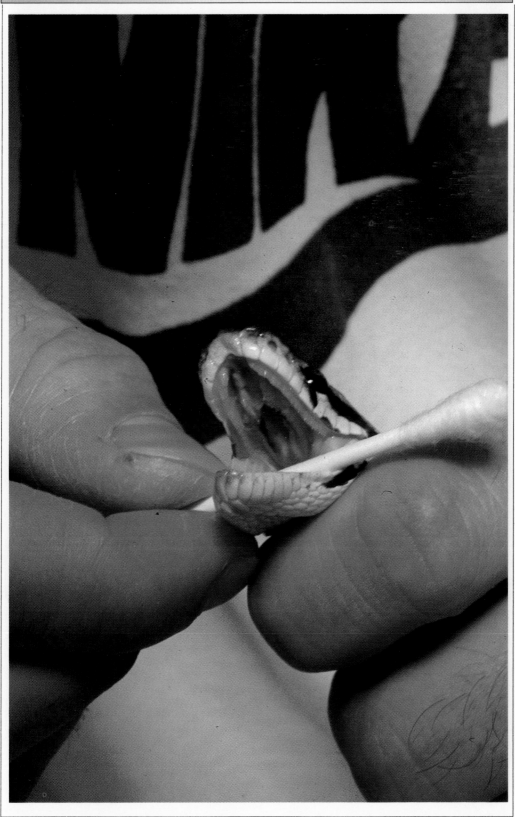

Protozoan Infections: Many enteric infections are caused by protozoa. If untreated, these diseases can rapidly reach epidemic proportions. Symptoms include watery, slimy feces, and general debilitation. Treatment with metronidazole (by a veterinarian) via stomach tube has proved effective.

Skin Problems: A common cause of skin infections in pythons is inability to slough properly, often as a result of a mite infestation or stress brought about by various other factors. Mite infestations should be

Any optical infections should be left to the capable hands of a veterinarian. In the case shown here, the eyes were already swollen when the snake was imported. Photo by Jim Merli.

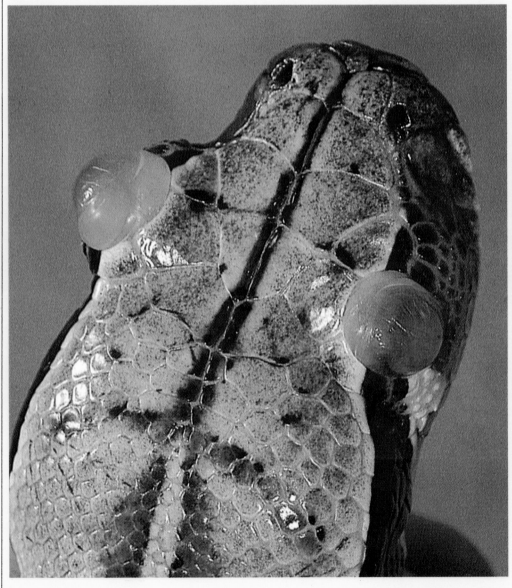

Mouth rot is one of the most common captive snake diseases. Signs include a swollen oral region, heavy and labored breathing, general lethargy, softening of the gums, and refusal of food. Mouth rot can lead to death and should be dealt with immediately. Photo by William B. Allen, Jr.

cleared immediately and aid should be given to snakes experiencing difficulty in sloughing. Most healthy pythons will slough (molt) their skins, problem-free, several times per year, a natural phenomenon related to growth. The skin is normally shed whole and the process should take no more than an hour or two at the most. Unhealthy skin caused by various factors may result in the skin coming away in patches. Disease organisms can grow behind persistent patches of old skin which do not come off readily. The skin can be loosened and peeled off by placing the reptile in a bath of very shallow, warm water for an hour or so.

Another infection of the body surface include abscesses, which appear as lumps below the skin. These are usually caused by infection building up in the flesh after the skin has been accidentally damaged for one reason or another. Abscesses should be treated by a veterinarian, who probably will give antibiotics. In severe cases the abscess may have to be surgically opened, cleaned up, and then sutured.

Respiratory Infections: Though relatively uncommon in Burmese Pythons, respiratory infections may occur occasionally in stressed specimens. The patient will have difficulty in breathing, the nostrils will be blocked, and there will be a nasal discharge. Often the symptoms can be alleviated by moving the patient to a warmer, drier, well-ventilated terrarium. More serious cases will require antibiotic treatment.

QUARANTINE

One of the most important means of keeping disease from your collection is to ensure that no diseases are brought in with new stock. That is why it is important for all new snakes to be given a period of quarantine before you introduce them to any existing snakes you may have.

Newly acquired snakes should be placed in a simple cage with minimum furnishings (a water bath, a hide box, and absorbent paper for the substrate being sufficient) and kept under close observation for 21 days. If no symptoms of illness appear during this time, you can safely assume that the snake is healthy and then give it normal accommodations. If not, or if you are unsure, you should get advice from your veterinarian or from a more experienced enthusiast.

Quarantine cages should be kept in a completely different room from the one in which your main stock is kept and you should maintain strict hygienic conditions, ensuring that you do nor transmit germs from your new snakes to your existing stock. Always wash hands thoroughly between each handling/cleaning session.

BURMESE PYTHON BREEDING

In these days of concern for the continuing existence of wildlife on our planet, it should be the duty all keepers of snakes (or indeed, any wildlife) to encourage their pets to reproduce. Many species are now almost impossible to obtain from the wild due not only to their increasing scarcity but also to international protective legislation. Keepers of particular species or races like the Burmese Pythons have a duty to keep captive stocks at a level that will meet demand. As herpetological interests are likely to continue to increase, there is every reason to believe that the demand for these animals will be greater in the future.

One unfortunate downside of this that gives us all concern is the fact that the relatively small captive gene pool has given rise to increasing anomalies that are very interesting from the scientific point of view but are not really esthetically desirable. While I am not totally against "color variety breeding" if applied in a sensible manner, I would really hate to see the morphology of snakes, including Burmese Pythons, manipulated genetically in the same fashion that it has been done with, say, dogs, many of which now show little or no evidence as to how they actually evolved. For this reason it is important that sooner or later we must try and initiate a pedigree system for various species. Studbooks would be a good start.

Burmese Pythons are commonly bred in captivity, probably because there are so few demands made on the keeper. Most interestingly, Burmese Pythons can reach sexual maturity at the age of 18 months. Photo by B. Kahl.

We should try to keep strict records of our breedings for the benefit of all python people now and in the future.

REPRODUCTION IN THE WILD

Male Burmese Pythons are ready to breed when about 6 ft 6 in/2 m; with females, its about 10 ft/3 m. Well-fed specimens can reach this size after two to three years, but for healthier results, it is recommended that the snakes are

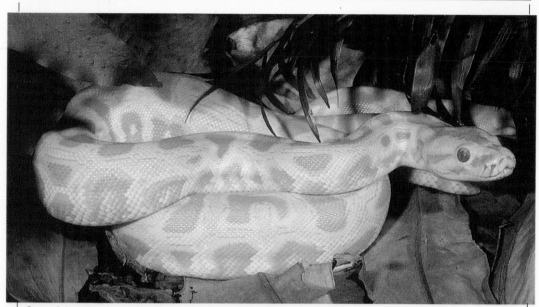

One of the most stunning products of selective Burmese Python breeding is the albino specimen. There are many albino Burmese Pythons available to the interested enthusiast, and their prices are usually quite reasonable. Photo by Mella Panzella.

fed moderately so that they do not become obese in their younger stages and reach the size for sexual maturity in three to four years.

It is thought that photoperiod has a direct influence on the sex drive and mating takes place in the winter as a result of a reduction in length of daylight. As the ancestors of most captive Burmese Pythons probably originated from Thailand or adjacent areas, temperature and/or humidity may also play a role. The main habitat of the Burmese Python in these areas is open woodland to dense forest, usually close to permanent water. There is a winter dry season and temperatures falling to not less than 50°F (10°C). In the summer, temperatures are usually well over 70°F (21°C) and rainfall is monsoonal.

Mating occurs usually during the months of December or January.

There is a plausible explanation for the timing of reproduction. Sexually mature snakes will still be well-fed and healthy after the previous warm season and thus be in top breeding condition. After copulation, the eggs develop in the maternal body for anything from 60 to 140 days. If copulation occurred in late December, this would mean that egglaying would occur in late-February to mid-May, at the beginning of the warmer, wetter season (ideal for egg incubation). Additionally, the young will hatch at a climatically favorable time (and when food prey will be abundant), giving the juveniles a good start in life and preparation for the winter rest period.

SEX DETERMINATION
The most obvious requirement for breeding is to have a male and a female. In adult snakes the male is

shorter (up to 10 ft/300 cm maximum) and generally more slender in form, while the female is longer (up to 20 ft/600 cm maximum) and generally more robust in form. In well-fed snakes it is quite easy to distinguish the sexes from about six months of age. However, it is not quite so easy in juveniles under 4 feet in length. This is best done with a sexing probe. The lubricated metal probe (available from specialist suppliers) is inserted into either side of the vent and pushed gently towards the tail tip. In females the probe can only be pushed the width of one or two subcaudal scales, while in males the probe will enter the inverted hemipenis at the base of the tail and can be pushed the equivalent of about ten subcaudal scales towards the tail tip.

BRINGING BURMESE PYTHONS INTO CONDITION

Wild Burmese Pythons are usually fairly solitary outside the breeding season and will therefore usually ignore chance meetings with the opposite sex. There is evidence to suggest that keeping

To determine the sex of a Burmese Python, you will have to "probe" the animal. Before inserting a sexing probe, you must coat it with some type of lubricant. Photo by Isabelle Francais, courtesy of Eugene L. Bessette.

Needless to say, some snakes don't care for probing very much, and thus it is best that two people handle the job; one to do the probing while the other holds the animal still. This is particularly important when probing very large specimens, who may not take kindly to the procedure and might deliver a nasty bite in response. Photo by Isabelle Francais, courtesy of Eugene L. Bessette.

Facing page: The initial step to probing any snake is to clean off the probe with alcohol. *Never* insert a probe that isn't sterile into a snake. Photo by Isabelle Francais, courtesy of Eugene L. Bessette.

the sexes separate until breeding time will increase chances of successful breeding, so you are advised to keep your males and your females separately.

Ensure your snakes are well fed throughout the summer and fall and, about mid November, start decreasing the photoperiod and temperature in the cage and stop feeding the snakes. Over a period of about one month, gradually reduce your maximum daytime temperature from 82°F/28°C to 68°F/20°C. At the same time, the period of lighting should be reduced from about 14 hours per day to 11 hours per day. Introduce females to males toward the end of your temperature/photoperiod reductions and you should get an almost immediate mating response. The females will have been affected by the environmental change and will have started to release vitellogin pheromones (sexual attractants) from areas between the scales. This pheromone will sexually arouse a male.

After crawling along the female's back with much jerking and tongue "tasting," the male gets into a position where he can push the rear part of his body under hers in order to get their cloacas in apposition. The receptive female will make it easy for the male to insert one of his hemipenes in her cloaca. Copulation can last

Facing page: Incubation containers can be just about anything. The use of clear plastic boxes in conjunction with many facets of herpetoculture has become very popular in recent years. Plastic products are, in many ways, very sensible. Photo by Isabelle Francais, courtesy of Eugene L. Bessette.

anything from a few minutes to several hours. During this time the snakes usually remain still while the sperm transfers from male to female.

After the pair separates the male can be left with the female for a week or so to allow for any successive matings. Then, after a couple of weeks, the male should be moved back to his own cage.

THE GRAVID FEMALE

Once fertilized, the female is said to be gravid. She will keep the eggs in her body for 60 to 140 days, usually about 70 to 80 days. After about 30 days of gravidity, the rear end of the female's abdomen takes on a plump appearance, and later the actual outline shape of the eggs can be seen. The snake will usually stop feeding after about the third week of gravidity, and will not feed again until the eggs hatch. A gravid snake should be handled as little as possible.

EGGLAYING

When ready, the female will lay her eggs somewhere on the cage floor. The eggs—which are about the size of a hen's, have a white, soft, leathery shell, and number from 25 to 60—are pushed into a cone-shaped pile by the female. Then she coils around them, fully covering them with her body. It is best to allow the female to incubate the eggs herself rather than take them away for artificial incubation. I, at least, have always had a higher hatch rate when I have left the eggs with the mother. Burmese

Although many pythons have the ability to incubate their own eggs, an amateur keeper should be aware that it is not standard procedure to allow the mothers near the newly hatched snakes. Although Burmese Pythons are not generally considered cannibalistic, it is simply not a good habit to get into. Photo by B. Kahl.

Pythons that are incubating their eggs are unique in the reptile world in being able to elevate their body temperature up to 7°F (12 to 13°C) above that of the surrounding environment.

The snake incubates the eggs for about 60 days, then they start to hatch. Usually not all of the eggs will hatch; some may have been infertile while others may have stopped developing somewhere along the way. You should expect 50 to 80% success at the very least. The mother will leave the eggs and return to her routine method of living as soon as hatching begins. After that she will show no further interest in her young. Allow each youngster to fully hatch before moving it to a separate cage.

REARING

The young will not feed until after the first molt, which is usually two to eight days after hatching. They are about 24 in/60 cm in length and quite capable of feeding on mice. For the first few months, one mouse per week should suffice. Young pythons should be tamed by frequent and regular handling (but not on feed day or the day following). The youngsters can be quite feisty and will bite readily but their teeth are too small to cause more than a few pricks through the skin. After just a few handling sessions they will stop this and will not bite again as long as they are regularly handled.

Facing page: For the truly advanced herpetoculturist, there are commercial incubators designed to accommodate the eggs of just about any creature. Isabelle Francais, courtesy Eugene L. Bessette. **Below:** The only drawback to commercial incubators is their price; these items are not cheap! However, they are reliable to the point of being almost foolproof, and thus if you are a commercial breeder with a lot of expensive stock to worry about, then the investment is undoubtedly worthwhile. Photo by Isabelle Francais, courtesy of Eugene L. Bessette.

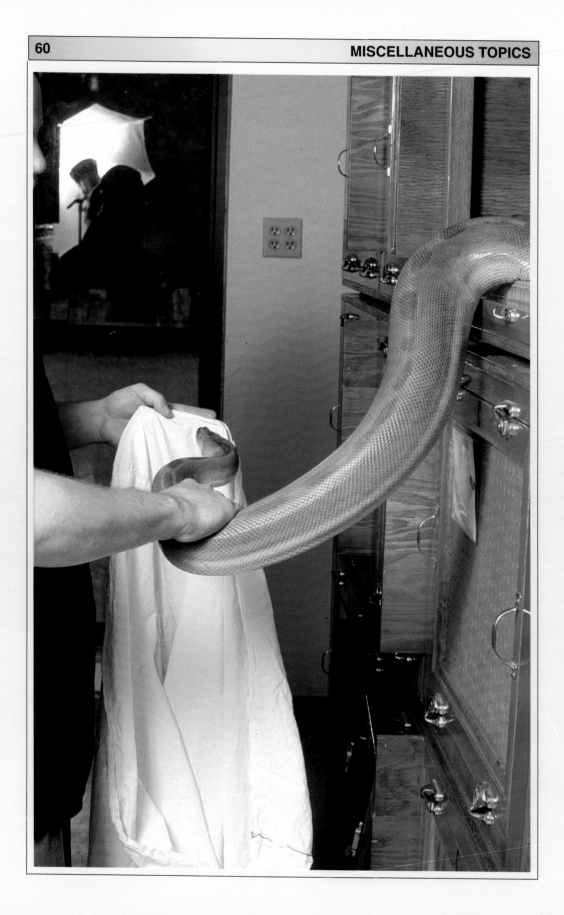

MISCELLANEOUS TOPICS

TRANSPORTING BURMESE PYTHONS

The most satisfactory method of carrying snakes, and one that has been used for many years, is to pack the reptiles individually in cloth bags. Strong cotton, drill, or linen is ideal, but strong pillow cases or rice sacks will usually do quite well. The serious enthusiast will always have a selection of bags of various sizes. A number of snakes in separate bags can be packed in partitions in large wooden or thick cardboard transport boxes. If the box has to travel during excessively cold weather it should be lined with an insulating material such as styrofoam. Always select the quickest and most direct route to your destination.

When purchasing new stock it is always best to pick it up yourself when convenient. Not only can you then inspect the snakes before you purchase them, you can also ensure they have a comfortable journey home. If travelling by car on a short journey in reasonably warm weather, it is usually quite okay to put the snake in a bag and on the floor of the car, but for longer

Facing page: The only Burmese Pythons that should be handled are those that you know are tame or very close to being tame. Very large and very hostile Burmese Pythons have, on more than one occasion, given their keepers wounds that required heavy bandaging and, in some cases, even stitches. Photo by Isabelle Francais, courtesy of Eugene L. Bessette.

or colder journeys you should place the bag(s) into a box or boxes.

Should you have to send any snakes by public transport or freightline, you must ensure that each individual bag is labelled, that the transport box is insulated, and that it is clearly marked with the name, address, and telephone number of the consignee, plus warning instructions to the effect that the crate should not be left outside in cold conditions.

HANDLING AND TAMING

It is necessary to handle your snakes frequently and regularly in order to tame them, to keep them tame, and at the same time to inspect them. Hatchling Burmese Python can usually be picked up with one hand, but until they are tame they will attempt to bite. At hatchling size, the bite is no worse than a few pin pricks, but it is still wise to avoid being bitten if you can, if only to save the snake's fragile teeth that are easily broken at this stage. To be on the safe side any bites can be simply wiped with a little antiseptic.

An untamed snake up to 3 ft/ 90 cm should be grasped firmly, but at the same time gently, just behind the head, allowing the body to drape across the hand and arm. With particularly lively specimens you will need to restrain the body with the other hand. Young snakes (the younger the better) are the easiest to tame and will usually become docile after a few handling sessions. After picking up the snake a few times behind the head, try releasing the head once the snake is comfortably entwined around your hand. Then you can rearrange the snake with your other hand as it moves about. If it continues to bite, wear a glove or wind a cloth around one hand and allow it to strike at that a few times. As the snake begins to realize how futile its actions are it will eventually stop striking.

Large untamed specimens, up to say 5 ft/150 cm in length, are more difficult. They must be secured behind the head with the whole of one hand and the body must be secured with the other. Bites from specimens of this size can be very painful so be very careful! A tame python of this size can simply be picked up with both hands, roughly one-third and two-thirds along its body. Then you can drape it over your arms and restrain it occasionally if it tries to crawl off.

Burmese Pythons in excess of 5 ft/150 cm can give a serious bite with their numerous long, thick, recurved teeth, and their constrictive powers must be treated with great respect. Specimens of this size that are untamed are never likely to become completely tame, even with regular handling, so such specimens are not suitable as pets

though they may be useful in breeding programs. A large aggressive Burmese Python should be handled by two people—one to get the snake firmly behind the head to prevent it biting and the other to hold the body to prevent it constricting. Do not allow the snake to get a grip on your arms, legs, or anywhere else for that matter! If it does, calmly unwind or get somebody to unwind it from the tail end first. When handled, untamed Burmese also have a habit of voiding the contents of the cloaca, which are not only evil-smelling but may also be quite corrosive to clothing. Remember, always wear old clothes during handling sessions. When dealing with large, untamed pythons, you should, for safety reasons, always ensure that another responsible person is within earshot. Also, never leave any large python with unsupervised children.

Hand-reared large Burmese will usually remain tame as long as they are handled frequently. As long as you are still capable of lifting such a snake, it can be draped about the shoulders and allowed to rest there. But remember, it may one day reach such a size and weight that you may no longer be able to pick it up and remember also that a constrictor doesn't even have to be as big as a Burmese Python to pose a definite danger to a person carrying it.

Burmese Pythons can be placed in cloth sacks for temporary transport. For longer trips, they should be further placed into sturdy containers of some kind (plastic sweaterboxes, large cardboard boxes, etc.). Photo by Isabelle Francais, courtesy of Eugene L. Bessette.

TW-128, 592 pgs, 1400+ color photos

TS-144, 208 pgs, 200+ photos & illus.

TS-194, 192 pgs, 175+ photos

TS-193, 736 pgs, 1400+ color photos

TS-189, 224 pgs, 180+ color photos

KW-127, 96 pgs, 80 color photos

TW-111, 256 pgs, 180+ color photos

AP-925, 160 pgs, 120 photos